The Squirrel's Finnegan

Written By J. Russell Brooks

Leavitt Peak Press

ISBN: 978-1-971940-14-4 (sc)
ISBN: 978-1-971940-11-3 (hc)
ISBN: 978-1-971940-15-1 (e)

Rev. date: 02/05/2026

Dedication Page

I dedicate this book to Troy, his
Family and all the other families
who have kids with special gifts.

Acknowledgement

A special thanks goes to Robin Gafa. She is an elementary school teacher that helped. immensely with the final edit of my children's book. Her insights and suggestions were invaluable to what I envisioned my story would be.

There once was a family of

Squirrels

named The Finnegan's;

Dad, Mom, Troy, and Sydney.

This is their story.

The Finnegan's were a small part of a large family filled with grandparents, moms and dads, aunts and uncles, sisters and brothers, and cousins. Robin was especially close to her twin sister Rhonda. They live in the suburbs of a big tree city named Chestnut City, of course Rhonda not far away just one town over. They had a beautiful house almost at the top of a tall oak tree. Joe and Robin were very happy. Joe worked very hard at the walnut cracking factory and Robin was a flight attendant for Tree Branch Airlines. Not long after Robin and Joe were married, they decided to have a family. Troy, their first born, had a very special gift known as Down Syndrome. Mom and Dad learned all about Down Syndrome knowing they would do all they could to help Troy develop his gifts. They both decided that it would be best for Troy if Mom stayed home to take care of him. Sadly, she left her career as a flight attendant. Mom and Dad found a doctor that specialized in the early development for children with Down Syndrome. Mom, Dad, and Troy started making trips twice a year to visit the doctor. The doctor's office was in Pecan Beach City and on these visits; the Finnegan's would visit their family friends, the Brooks'.

The families were reunited when

would come to Pecan Beach City for Troy's doctor appointments.
Russ Brooks had been a friend to Troy's Mom
and Aunt Rhonda since they were children in high school together. It was not long before
Russ was known as Uncle Russ and his mom Joan was known as Grammy Joan. The families
enjoyed spending time together in Grammy Joan's condo on the Chesapeake Bay.

Just over a year after Troy was born another bundle of joy was added to the family, a girl named Sydney. She was born without Troy's gift but was very special in her own way. The Finnegan's continued their family visits to Pecan Beach City. The doctor at each visit measured Troy's progress and concluded his gift of Down syndrome was mild. A few years passed; Sydney was around three and already seemed to understand that Troy was a special kid. The Finnegan's, being very happy in their home and were often seen playing in their front lawn, Troy crawling and Sydney scampering from branch to branch. Sydney loved her brother, and she knew she would always be by his side to protect him. Sydney was already walking and talking and wondered why Troy was not able to yet. She also noticed when her family all went into town adults would stare at Troy with sad expressions on their faces. Other children would just stare or look frightened. Sydney asked her mom why. Mom said,

"Troy has a very special brain that learns things just a little slower."

She went on further to explain,

"Since Troy looks different than most squirrels, they just get curious as to why".

Sawyer seemed to understand her mother's explanation but could not shake the mad feelings she would get when other squirrels would stare at her big brother.

Most of the Finnegan's neighbors were very friendly, except for the family three doors down. The Crocks, a family of flying squirrels. The two boys Jason and Jackson were a couple of years older than Troy. The Crocks thought they were better than everybody because they could

fly.

Jason and Jackson thought this most of all.

It was a beautiful summer day, many of the neighborhood children were outside playing. Jason and Jackson started flying over Troy's head, they were calling him mean names. Troy at the time did not understand and thought it was fun watching the boys fly so close to his head. Sydney on the other hand, knew something was wrong. She ran into the house to get her mom. Sydney told her mom what the boys were calling Troy. With Sydney clinging to her, Mom quickly stepped out onto the stoop. Before she could even say a word, Jason and Jackson flew away. Troy looking no worse for wear continued laughing as the boys dropped out of sight.

Soon after, Dad got home from work and gave his family kisses and big hugs. After dinner and the kids were in bed Mom told Dad that the Crock boys had been bullying Troy. As a protective father, Dad's first reaction was to go to the Crock home and confront the boy's parents. Mom and Dad both sadly knew that because Troy looked different, that this would not be the last time he was bullied. Mom and Dad decided not to confront the Crock family knowing it would not be the last time Troy will have to deal with bullies. Knowing they could do very little to help the situation. They decided instead to help Troy better understand the world around him.

Since the day Troy was born, Mom and Dad and the whole extended family for that matter knew that the special gifts Troy was born with would require certain demands to assure he have as normal a life as possible. Troy and kids like him born with special gifts find it more difficult to learn as fast as kids not born with special gifts. Even though Troy was born different, the whole Finnegan family felt unconditional love for him. They just knew they were up for any and all challenges his special gifts would require.

Mom and Dad knew Troy's special gifts would require them to focus extra time and effort to him. So when Sydney was born, they made a pact that they would set aside quality time devoted to just her. It is hard for most families to understand the extra effort that it takes to raise a child with special gifts; but once you experience that innocent, unconditional love they give, it all seems more than worth it.

Troy was six now and no longer needed to visit the doctor in Pecan Beach City. The family continued to visit and stay with Grammy Joan and Uncle Russ. Grammy Joan and Uncle Russ also started to visit the Finnegan's at their home in Chestnut City. Both the Finnegan's neighborhood and Grammy Joan's condo had swimming pools, so swimming was always a part of the Finnegan's lives. Whenever they would come to Grammy Joan's she would have activities planned for each day. But by the end of the day, everyone would all end up in the pool together. Dad taught both Sydney and Troy to swim free style, breaststroke, backstroke, and butterfly. To everyone's amazement, Troy took to the water like a fish, he would do hundreds of laps until he was forced to get out of the

The next fall, it was time for

Sydney and Troy to go to school.

Mom and dad had spent all summer teaching the kids

how to react to bullies. Mom and Dad said,

"try to ignore them and not shout back mean names, but most importantly if the bullies try to touch you in any way, run to the nearest adult for protection."

Sydney did not think this seemed to be brave but listened to her parents.

Sydney knew she would be there to protect Troy however she could.

One of the very first days on the school bus, a couple of kids tried to be mean to Troy. But cleverly, Troy and Sydney pretended the bullies didn't exist. After getting no reaction from Troy or Sydney most of the bullies on the bus just gave up and left Troy to sit in peace.

Sydney adjusted to school quickly, liking her teacher and making new friends with her classmates. Troy struggled in his classes having to work twice as hard as the other kids; his special brain just was not able to learn as fast. Troy had one class that was designed especially for kids with special gifts. Kids just like Troy were in this class. Troy was amazed because he had never seen other kids that looked like him before. At first, he did not know how to act.

In Troy's class the kids worked on how to speak more clearly.
They learned how to behave and react to other kids and adults. Troy's
favorite subject was math, and he did well. He was learning to read, but
like a lot of other kids, he had trouble with his comprehension.
For the next few years, both Troy and Sydney did well in elementary school.
There was always a hint of teasing from some students and even so it made
Troy feel angry sometimes. He remembered that his parents taught him to be
a better person and ignore them. Mom and Dad worked closely with the school
to help shield Troy and the other special kids from bad behavior and bullying.
Mom, Dad, Sydney, and Troy realized that bullies must pick on others to feel
better about themselves. Though school took priority, both kids really got into
sports, baseball, basketball, and of course, swimming! Dad, being athletic
himself he would get a fatherly gleam in his eyes every time
one of his kids would get a hit or sink a basket.

Mom saw how much Troy enjoyed playing sports. So, mom
got him involved in the local Special Olympics.

Troy did very well in swimming and running.

The whole family was at every event cheering Troy on. Troy loved the Special
Olympics because he was able to compete with other kids born with special gifts.
The Special Olympics was not only good for Troy, but for Mom and Dad too. Mom
and Dad found the Special Olympics to be a haven where they could talk to other
parents with kids that had special gifts. They were able to get and give good advice
about ideas and programs that have helped with the challenges of raising kids with
special gifts. Grammy Joan made many trips to Chestnut City to come watch Troy.
She was there during one of the Special Olympics events to see Troy run track.
Back at school, Sydney had become quite the athlete too. She even made
the school's basketball team. All the girls on the team took a shine
to Troy and let him help at some practices and games. He had his own
team uniform and walked around like he was the assistant coach.

It was Troy and Sydney's last year of elementary school. Mom and Dad were growing worried about the bullying they knew went on in middle school. They chose to send both kids to private school which can be very expensive. Even though Tom had worked his way up to production manager at the walnut cracking factory and was making more money, the added expense of private school would make things tough. Money was going to be tight and they grateful to family members contributing to the cost of the school. Mom and Dad were used to the financial challenges they had to bare raising children and were willing to make any sacrifices to insure Troy and Sydney would have a bright future. Sydney thrived at private schools and made the cheer squad and basketball team. But Troy struggled. The classes were just too advanced for him, and it took two more schools before Mom found a school that would be the right fit for him. It was amazing how Robin was able to juggle endless doctor's appointments, carpools, homework, and meals over the years, but she did. Every time Uncle Russ would come for a visit, he was so impressed with how Robin and Joe worked as a team to take care of Sydney and Troy. The Finnegan's were like a well-oiled machine, but like any other family, that can be stressful on a marriage. Over the years, Grammy Joan and Uncle Russ noticed some difficulties between Mom and Dad but saw that they never let emotions get in the way of caring for their kids.

Troy and Sydney were on the neighborhood swim team, and Uncle Russ came to visit one summer. He went to their swimming competitions. Sydney and Troy both swam like fish and did well at the competitions. The lifeguards loved Troy, making him an honorary guard. He would walk around the pool helping the guards enforce the pool rules on the younger kids. It was so nice being in a public place where everyone knew Troy and there were no long stares or whispered comments.

Uncle Russ often contemplated over the years about how much the bullies in Troy's life had missed. Their quick judgment made them miss out on a friendship with a great kid. It wasn't just kids that prejudged Troy's special gifts. Once when Troy was at reading class, a mother walked in the classroom and saw her son and Troy reading a book. The mother approached the teacher concerned that Troy would slow down her son's studies. The teacher, with a little smirk on her face, informed the mother that Troy was helping her son get caught up on his reading assignments.

Mom was always trying to find special experiences for Troy and the family. They had all become avid fans of the Chestnut City Braves and had attended a few games. One day Mom contacted the team manager and told him all about Troy and her family. He invited the Finnegan's to the next home game and had Troy assist with the first pitch! With Mom, Dad, and Sydney sitting in the Brave's dugout, they watched Troy on the mound with the pitcher waiting for the catcher's call. The crowd roared in laughter when Troy shrugged off the catcher's first signal. The next one was to Troy's satisfaction. With microphone in hand, he turned to the pitcher and said,

"Let her rip"!

The crowd cheered as Troy ran off the field beaming with pride.

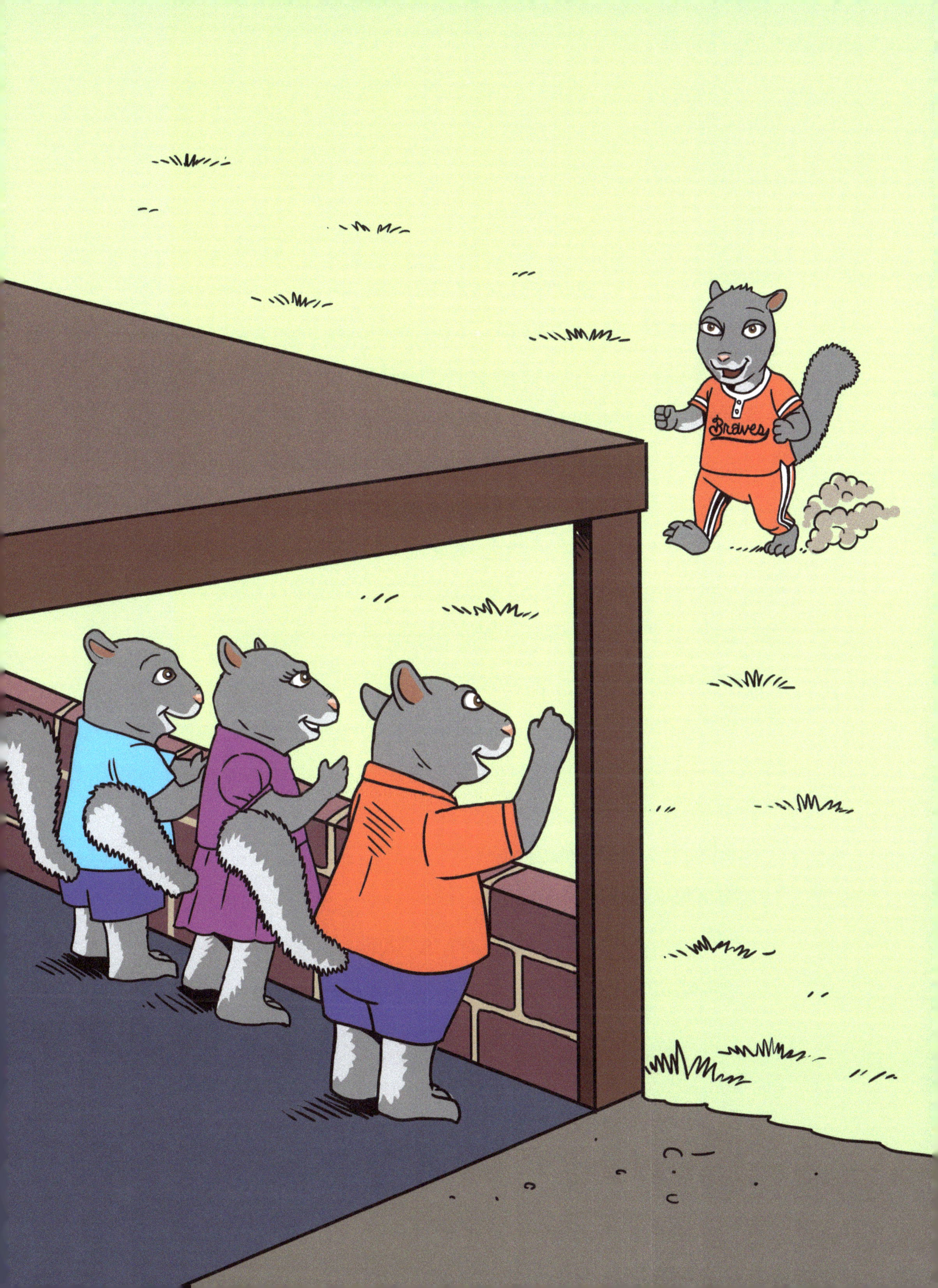
Braves

As a child, Troy had a huge Matchbox car collection that he could play with for hours. He was always good at entertaining himself, which was great for Mom because it would give her some much-needed down time. After the Match Box cars, it was Bingo. The family played almost every night and Troy was always the caller. Over the years, Troy's math skills just got better and better, and he had a talent for remembering dates. You could tell him anyone's birthday and he would remember it and be able to tell you the day of the week it would be on next year. Even if Troy hadn't seen someone for a few years, he would remember their birthday. The Finnegan's, like everyone else, fell prey to the latest electronic gadgets, laptops, cell phones, video games, etc. Bah Hum Bug Uncle Russ even came for Christmas one time and was impressed at Troy's skills on all the different electronics. Troy still liked to spend time alone, but his new entertainment was listing related words and solving tough math problems on a dry erase board. Watching Troy and Sydney growing up always amazed Uncle Russ. He was proud of how Sydney had matured faster than Troy, but she always made time to play with him. As a young teen, Sydney had many girlfriends and made sure to include Troy in their activities whenever she could.

One year, when Troy was in middle school, Mom and Dad had a big decision to make. Troy had to stay back a year to improve on some of the skills in which he was behind.

Sydney and Troy were now prepared for high school. It was getting more difficult to pay for private school. Mom and Dad decided to keep Sydney in a private school and send Troy to public high school. Mom as usual did her research and found a high school that had a very good program for kids with special gifts. Mom and Dad did not make the decision lightly, but knew the reality was they would not be around forever. They knew Sydney at some point would become Troy's primary care giver. Unfortunately, parents of kids with special gifts are confronted by these kinds of concerns all the time.

Soon after Troy started high school, mom got a job working with Troy and the other kids with special gifts. The job not only helped the family financially but gave her a bird's eye view of how Troy was advancing in school. Troy was just about a month into his sophomore year in high school when the captain of the football team, Travis, spotted him in the cafeteria. Travis remembered Troy from the Chestnut City Braves game where Troy assisted with the first pitch of the game. Travis was so impressed with Troy's performance; he knew he had to get to know this kid. Now Travis was not your typical high school football player. He was kind, aware, and interested in getting to know a kid that was so different from himself. Travis was at the top of his class academically and a great athlete as well. He was well respected by the high school staff and looked up to by most of the students. Troy and Travis first met at the pep rally for the first football game of the season. Troy was his innocent, charming self, and Travis took an immediate liking to him. Travis' and Troy's love for all things sports made them, although an odd one, a match made in heaven. Travis talked to his teammates and coaches and said, "You have to meet this kid!".

Mom was so excited by the interest Travis had for Troy, she soon welcomed him to their family's circle of trust. It was not long before Troy was meeting Travis' fellow teammates and coaches. Troy's always happy demeanor and knowledge of sports won the hearts of the players and coaches. First the football team, then followed by the basketball and baseball teams where Troy was named honorary assistant coach. Troy would sit with the teams cheering the players on. He always had his dry erase board handy to keep his stats on the games. Troy truly inspired the whole high school and broke a lot of the stereotypes about kids with special gifts. Troy's notoriety in high school pleasantly meant he did not have many bullying incidents to deal with. Mom, Dad, Sydney and Aunt Rhonda come to as many games as possible and cheer with pride for Troy and the teams. Travis had become like a big brother to Troy and Sydney and was a welcomed member of the Finnegan family. Mom and Dad were so grateful for all that Travis brought to Troy's high school experience. The family was heartbroken when he graduated and left for college.

Sydney continued to thrive at private schools. Her grades were great, and she

was making lots of new friends. She was going to dances and having sleepovers.

She made the basketball team again, and as usual, Troy was at

every game assuming his assistant coaching role.

The entire team fawned over him. The coaches were always giving him sportsman

slaps on the butt telling him what a great job he was doing. Troy was in his

element out on the floor and was destined for bigger things at his own school.

Life was very good for the Finnegan's. Although they struggled financially, Mom and Dad always made sure the kids were secure and happy. Sydney and Troy were both starting their senior year in high school. The whole family had become sports enthusiasts, watching whatever game, match or meet was on television at the time. When Uncle Russ visited, he had the idea of teaching Troy how to work with Excel, a math program on the computer. This was a wonderful idea because Troy loved numbers and math. Uncle Russ showed Troy how to create spreadsheets. They even made one into a calendar so Troy could play with all the dates and birthdays he had roaming around in that big brain of his. Dad continued to teach Troy how to use

It was not long after that Troy got his first job at the local hardware store helping with inventory counts for the entire store. He got to interact with the customer, which really helped improve his social skills. There were a few customers that shied away from Troy, but most would engage him in small talk and found they were always greeted with bright happy kid.

Sydney got her driver's license in her sophomore year and was running household errands to help Mom out. The family did not know what kind of explanation they would tell Troy if he asked why he could not get his driver's license, but he had not brought it up. He just loved getting to spend time alone with Sydney when she drove him to work. Sydney on the other hand, did not have time for a job between being on the lacrosse team, captain of the basketball team, and her other extracurricular activities. She hardly had time to sleep. By far, her favorite activity was the broadcast club. Sydney had already decided that she wanted to study television network broadcasting in college and become a famous female sportscaster. She received several basketball scholarship offers to college. Mom and Dad could not be any prouder of their kids. Parents always want to see their children blossom into successful young adults. Mom and Dad worried about Troy because of his special gifts and were uncertain about his future. Their worries seemed to be over for the time being, (not that a parent's worries are ever over). Both Troy and Sydney were graduating from high school. Sawyer had earned a basketball scholarship to Chestnut City University. The entire Finnegan Family and of course Grammy Joan and Uncle Russ were at Troy and Sydney's graduations. There were tons of proud tears and happy laughs while Troy and Sydney celebrated their graduation with family and friends.

The summer passed by quickly, and it was time for Sydney to leave for college. Mom, Dad, Troy, and Aunt Rhonda, (who was always there at every event: birthdays, holidays, games, illnesses, or just because) were there to see Sydney off. The tears from all were flowing and Troy, sitting in sister's car, declared he was going to college with her. Sydney gave him a long tight hug and said that he had his own college to go to and that they could talk on the phone every day. Troy stayed home with Mom and Dad and took the city bus to Chestnut Community College.

It just goes to show if enough love and selfless determination are given to a child; special gifts or not, can flourish and lead a happy fulfilling life.

About The Author

The author grew up in the 1960s as part of a Navy family, the youngest of three children. His father was a navy combat jet pilot where his career demanded him to move his family back forth across the country several times. The author was born in Pensacola, Florida but if you ask where he's from, he will tell you the United States. His family finally settled down in Virginia Beach, Virginia in 1972. Brooks was going into the eighth grade for what then was a five-year stretch in high school. He had always thrived in school, never having to work too hard. He was always very athletic and succeeded in both wrestling and gymnastics. His athletic passion now is big sailboat racing where he works the cockpit on a thirty-seven-foot sailboat. By day, Brooks works as an asset manager for a large car rental company and by night he mostly watches television, and even admits he is addicted to hour long drama series. When he was in his early fifties, his doctor diagnosed him as having signs of depression. With the doctor's help to manage his depression the author was inspired to write his first book: a memoir showcasing the ups and downs of his life. He'd hoped to inspire others that might have had similar life trials to seek out help as well. The inspiration and admiration for a lifelong friend and her family has motivated the author to write this children's book as a tribute to them.

www.ingramcontent.com/pod-product-compliance
Lightning Source LLC
Chambersburg PA
CBHW041127120626

46547CB00019B/2891